INSTITUTIONALISING MENTORSHIP IN THE LEGAL PROFESSION

A Strategic Blueprint for Professional Development

By

Hon. Justice Mabel T. Segun Bello
Judge of the Federal High Court of Nigeria.

Author: Hon. Justice Mabel T. Segun -Bello

ISBN- (Paperback) : 978-1-917267-66-3

ISBN- (E-Book) : 978-1-917267-67-0

Year Published - 2025

Independently Published : Hon. Justice Mabel T. Segun -Bello

Dedication

To every lawyer who once walked uncertain through the corridors of justice and to every mentor whose light made the way clear.

May our profession never lack wisdom, nor our generations lack guides.

Foreword

The strength of any profession lies not in its rules but in the character of those who live by them. The Nigerian legal profession has, for generations, distinguished itself by intellect and courage, yet every generation faces the same test whether it can transmit its values to those who follow. Without that transmission, learning decays into cleverness and integrity into nostalgia.

Hon. Justice Mabel Segun Bello, in this extraordinary work, has offered our profession both a mirror and a map. Institutionalising Mentorship in the Legal Profession: A Strategic Blueprint for Professional Development is not another treatise on ethics or procedure; it is a design for continuity. It shows, with clarity and compassion, that mentorship is not a sentimental luxury but a structural necessity the quiet engine through which judgment, discipline, and courage pass from one lawyer to another.

Any reader of this book would be impressed by its balance. It is scholarly yet human, visionary yet practical; it honours our traditions and the communal guidance of our professional forebears while speaking directly to the present realities of practice, technology, and the economic pressures that shape modern advocacy. It does what great legal writing should do: it calls us to memory and to responsibility.

The judiciary, the Bar, and the academy all have their places in this design. We must now move from rhetoric to architecture, from individual goodwill to institutional will. This blueprint gives us the tools to do so with clear principles, feasible frameworks, and a vision large enough to hold every segment of our profession.

I commend this book to every judge, every advocate, every teacher of law, and every student of law. It is a manual for reform and If we take its lessons seriously, we will renew not only our institutions but also the moral tenets that makes law a calling rather than a trade.

May this work inspire the Nigerian legal profession to become once more what it has always aspired to be: a community that learns together, serves together, and endures together.

Hon. Justice John Terhemba Tsoho.

Chief Judge.

Federal High Court of Nigeria.

Preface

The journey through the legal profession is as demanding as it is noble. From the first day at the University, to law school and to the practicing years, each lawyer carries not only the duty to interpret and apply the law but also the silent responsibility to guide others along its path. Mentorship, in the context of this book, is not a mere courtesy of the senior to the junior; it is the moral spine of our professional heritage which must now be institutionalised.

Over the years, I have observed with growing concern that mentorship in the Nigerian legal profession has become increasingly informal, and at times, incidental. Many young lawyers navigate the labyrinth of practice without consistent guidance, while some senior colleagues, burdened by professional pressures, overlook their duty to nurture successors. This book emerges from that observation—born of both reflection and conviction—that our profession must rediscover and establish the culture of deliberate, institutional mentorship.

The ideas presented here do not seek to impose new burdens, but to revive old virtues: diligence, humility, and ethical consistency. They propose a strategic framework that repositions mentorship as a regulated, measurable, and integral component of legal development—one that serves both the mentor and the mentee, and ultimately, strengthens the justice system.

This work draws inspiration from experiences within our courts, law schools, and Bar associations. It also draws from my own journey—one marked by the generosity of mentors who shaped not only my intellect but my values and character. Their patience, candour, and example were lessons no textbook could teach. It is my hope that every reader will see in these pages a call to emulate such stewardship.

Our profession stands at a critical intersection of reform. If we are to sustain its dignity, we must build systems that preserve wisdom and transmit values. May this book serve as both a blueprint and a reminder—that the measure of a great lawyer is not in the cases won, but in the lives shaped through guidance, integrity, and service.

— Hon. Justice Mabel T. Segun Bello
Federal High Court of Nigeria

Acknowledgments

Every work of scholarship is the product of many minds and generous spirits. I wish to acknowledge, first and foremost, my colleagues at the **Federal High Court of Nigeria**, whose intellectual rigour and sense of purpose continually remind me of the sacredness of our calling. Their daily dedication to justice and their constant readiness to provide guidance and supply encouragement to younger Judges, reinforces my belief that mentorship is not optional; it is an ethical necessity.

I owe deep gratitude to the **Nigerian Bar Association**, particularly its present leadership and the various continuing professional development committees, for sustaining the dialogue on mentorship, inclusivity and ethics in legal practice. Their commitment to the professional welfare of lawyers across the nation has been both inspiring and instructive.

Finally, I dedicate this work to every mentor who once saw promise in a young lawyer—and to every young lawyer who still believes that the law can be both a career and a calling. May this book strengthen the bridge between them.

About the Author

Hon. Justice Mabel Taiye Segun-Bello, presently serves as a Judge of the **Federal High Court of Nigeria**, where she has distinguished herself through a record of an unwavering commitment to adjudication.

Her legal career spans diverse spheres of practice—civil litigation, corporate law, and judicial administration—reflecting a lifelong dedication to both the study and practice of law.

In the year 2004 She had a brief stay in the banking sector where she was a Credit Administration/ Loan Recovery Officer – of a Bank.

Prior to her appointment as a Judge, she worked as a Magistrate and District Court Judge with the FCT (Fed. Capital Territory); High Court of Justice Abuja, Nigeria for a period of 18 years. Where she rose to the position of a Chief Magistrate in the year 2015 and ultimately was appointed a Deputy Chief Registrar and the Director for Oaths of the FCT High Court Abuja in the year 2021.

As the Director for oaths, Justice Mabel T. Segun-Bello pioneered the First Ever Digital Affidavit Registry Management System (ARMS). The first ever to be successfully done in the of the Nigerian Judiciary.

Justice Mabel Segun-Bello is an Associate member of the–Chartered Institute of Arbitrators and an Associate member of the Institute of Chartered Mediators and Conciliators (ICMC)

Beyond the courtroom, Justice Mabel is also a Conference speaker and training facilitator. An advocate for professional mentorship, continuing legal education, and the empowerment of young lawyers. She has been a keynote speaker at several national and regional legal conferences, including leadership conferences where she consistently emphasizes the importance of mainstreaming mentorship and leadership in the institutions, and generational continuity in the legal profession.

Her philosophy rests upon the conviction that law must be both learned and lived, and that every lawyer bears a duty to guide the next. Through her writings, rulings, and mentorship initiatives, she continues to contribute meaningfully to the growth of Nigeria's legal and judicial systems.

She is currently pursuing a postgraduate degree in International Economic Law, with a focus on the role of the ECOWAS Community Court of Justice in trade dispute resolution in West Africa.

This commitment to expanding her knowledge base, exemplifies her passion for staying at the forefront of Legal developments, leadership capital development, Nation Building, and driving positive change.

Table of Contents

CHAPTER ONE

The Spirit of Legal Mentorship — A Forgotten Tradition?

1. Why Mentorship Sits at the Heart of Our Profession

I have long believed that law is learned twice: first from books, and then from people. Books supply the scaffolding; mentors breathe flesh and life into the structure. In courtrooms and law chambers across Nigeria, the best habits of our craft—clear thinking, ethical restraint, courage under pressure—are not merely taught, they are transmitted. Mentorship is the medium of that transmission. When it thrives, the profession's conscience is audible; when it withers, our rules grow louder because our conscience grows faint.

Mentorship, as I use the term, is not a loose friendship between senior and junior. It is a structured relationship devoted to professional formation: the methodical transfer of, craft, ethical practices, conventions and responsibility from one generation to the next. And when this is Properly institutionalised, it is a public good for the business of law practice—**because better lawyers do not only win cases; they strengthen justice.**

When I first joined the Bar in the year 2001, the idea of being "under" a senior was neither humiliating nor optional; it was a recognised stage of professional formation. To learn was to sit near, to observe, to listen. Today, the pace of practice and the weight of survival have compressed that space. Senior lawyers rarely have the time, and juniors rarely have the proximity. The bond that once transmitted the profession's conscience now flickers in fragments.

2. Historical Roots: From Rhetoric to Reasoned Duty
"Mentor" – A word or a Name?

The word "mentor" originates from a character in Homer's ancient Greek poem, The Odyssey, written around 800 B.C.E. In the poem, the hero Odysseus entrusts his son, Telemachus, to the care and guidance of his trusted friend Mentor while he was away at war. The goddess of wisdom, Athena, frequently takes the form of Mentor and disguised herself as Mentor to guide Telemachus on his journey of self-discovery, in order to provide guidance, advice, and support to Telemachus, solidifying the name's association with wisdom and mentorship and making the name Mentor, synonymous with wise counsel and guidance.

• Modern Meaning: Due to this story, the name "Mentor" evolved and developed into a "common noun" representing a trusted counselor or guide who provides support and knowledge to a less experienced person.

Historical Legal Roots

Long before the common law matured, legal learning grew around masters. In Athens, students gathered to learn rhetoric as a civic duty; in Rome, young advocates observed jurists in the Forum and imitated their reasoned style. The method and formulae were: **proximity, practice, and correction.**

The English common law made this method enduring through the Inns of Court. Through the system of Pupillage novices were bound to seasoned counsel under an ethic that valued both competence and character. This ethic migrated and met African traditions that had long prized tutelage through community.

The result, in Nigeria, was not simple adoption but creative fusion: a formal apprenticeship layered over a communal culture of guidance.

3. The Inns of Court: Structured Teaching

When I first studied the history of the Inns of court, one lesson stood out: structured teaching. from Dining, to moot trials, readings, and pupillage. All these converted aspirations into habit. Supervisors were appointed and made accountable for a pupil's growth; pupils were expected to demonstrate progress, not merely attendance.

The Inns of Court began to gradually take on the responsibility of educating aspiring lawyers. They developed a formal system of training and governance, with a governing body of experienced members called "Masters of the Bench" or "Readers".

The four surviving Inns—Inner Temple, Middle Temple, Lincoln's Inn, and Gray's Inn—took their names from the properties they occupied. Over time, they became the sole providers of training for barristers, while the Inns of Chancery developed in response to the needs of other legal professionals like attorneys and solicitors.

Their Bar Standards Board's modern oversight reflects the old idea that—**mentorship is most reliable when the profession treats it as a duty, and not a favour.**

It is quite intriguing that Nigeria inherited these titles and procedures more readily and seriously than the mentoring discipline. We retained and codify the language of chambers, juniors, and senior counsel, legal maxims etc. but we did not codify expectations around mentorship formation. **This gap is the central theme of this book.**

4. Indigenous African Parallels: Guidance as Stewardship

Our continent also knew mentorship by other names. In Yoruba communities, the Baálẹ̀ and council of elders taught through role-modeling and repetition. In Igbo jurisprudence, the onye ndu—leader-guide—embodied the ethic that "I am because we are." Across the North, Emirs and councils balanced adjudication with administration. The method was public: the younger learned by watching the older resolve disputes with patience, proportion and equanimity.

This heritage matters. It reminds us that mentorship is not an imported technique; it is native to our moral construct. **The challenge is not to persuade Nigerians that guidance is good. It is to redesign institutions so that guidance is dependable and institutionalised.**

5. Early Nigeria: When the Bar Was simply a Small School

Oral histories have it that, the early post-independence Bar was a community where seniors personally groomed juniors. Work drafts sent by juniors to seniors returned with red ink and quiet lectures. Court visits were schooling, not errands. Many of our most admired senior legal practitioners were produced by such intentional tutelage and pupillage. What kept standards high was not only talent, but proximity, practice and correction: —daily exposure to the craft as practiced by those determined to intentionally pass it on.

As the profession expanded, this professional intimacy became harder. We multiplied numbers without multiplying methods. However, what was not learned is that - **Growth is not the enemy of mentorship; unplanned growth is.**

6. The Invisible Curriculum of Lawyering

Every profession has a hidden curriculum—the unwritten lessons and invisible conventions that shape conduct. In law, it includes: how to frame an issue; when to concede; how to write with restraint; how to speak with courage without provoking the court; the art of effective cross examination, pretrial skills, how to lead a client away from unlawful shortcuts and so on. These cannot be ingested from rules and books alone. They must be caught from seniors who practice what they preach. **In legal practice, more is caught than is taught through the books.**

The **Rules of Professional Conduct for Legal Practitioners (2023)** outline principles of integrity, courtesy, and fidelity, but without mentorship to embody these values, they remain aspirational. **Hence, a rule, without a model becomes a ruse. Mentorship is how we turn aspiration to manifestation and ultimately shape character.**

7. What Mentorship Actually Transfers (And Why It Matters)

(a) Epistemic judgment. Books teach what the law is; mentors teach what the law requires. The difference is in judgment— the ability to make considered decisions and arrive at sensible conclusions - how to choose among plausible paths under pressure.

(b) Ethical muscle. Professional Integrity and dignity is strengthened by making repeated, supervised choices. A senior who refuses a dubious brief teaches a junior both law and backbone.

(c) Professional identity formation. Belonging to a profession means you are ready to inhabit its best traditions and practices. **Mentorship aid's identity formation and inducts the younger lawyer into a narrative larger than personal ambition.**

(d) Social capital leverage (with responsibility). Access opens doors; responsibility keeps one worthy to walk through them. Capacity opens the door but integrity and responsible behavior keeps one in the room. A mentor lends both, and insists they be used well.

8. The Loosened Grip: The Quiet Drift and Slow Unravelling

There are losses that happen suddenly — a building collapses, a judgment is overturned — and there are those that erode quietly until only traces remain. The decline of mentorship in our profession belongs to the second kind. It has not been the work of villains or deliberate neglect; it has been the sum of small omissions repeated across decades, each too minor to provoke alarm, yet together strong enough to loosen the foundations of a proud tradition. This slow unravelling can be charted in phases.

I have watched, with deep concern, five forces that loosened and unravelled mentorship's grip:

<u>Socio-Economic Pressure.</u> The economic realities confronting many young lawyers further complicate mentorship. Poor remuneration, lack of structured welfare, and unrealistic work expectations leave little room for long-term professional reflection. The result is a culture of short-term survival: many juniors leave private practice prematurely for corporate roles, politics, or entrepreneurship. In this exodus, the cycle of mentorship is truncated. A profession that fails to nurture its youngest members loses not only its continuity but also its conscience. Economic pressure also distorts priorities. Junior lawyers, underpaid and overworked, often juggle multiple briefs for survival. Their concern is to meet deadlines, not to cultivate depth. Senior lawyers, facing operational costs and client expectations, focus on deliverables. Both sides begin to see mentorship as a luxury of calmer times. The paradox is painful: precisely when mentorship is most needed—it becomes least available.

<u>Numbers without systems.</u> Too many law graduates, fewer structured mentoring pathways. **This is called expansion without preparation**. The legal education system grew faster than the mentorship ecosystem that sustained it. When the numbers multiplied, the structure of apprenticeship did not.

<u>Digital distance.</u> Remote work improves flexibility, but weakens organic observation. The digital transformation of legal work, while offering efficiency, has unintentionally diminished the organic spaces where mentorship once flourished. The transition from chambers filled with books, arguments, and collective drafting sessions to solitary virtual offices has altered the social texture of legal learning. E-mails and online platforms cannot replicate the subtle lessons learned through shared work—the measured tone of a senior in court, the handwritten corrections on a draft affidavit, the pause before a submission. Again, I repeat - Mentorship thrives in proximity, practice and correction. Digitization, though powerful, often breeds isolation. It was once the norm that a junior would linger after court to seek counsel or observe a mentor's methods, today's lawyer prefers the anonymity of online research and the efficiency of virtual practice. The legal profession, however, is not sustained by knowledge alone but by example—and example requires presence. **Technological transformation** brought efficiency but diluted presence. Drafts travel by email; arguments are rehearsed over screens; feedback, when it comes, is terse and transactional. The hidden lessons — tone, patience, professional bearing

— cannot travel through fiber optic cables. **We have become connected but less accompanied.**

<u>Generational mistrust</u>. Generational gap can create generational mistrust. Seniors perceive impatience; juniors perceive indifference. Both will ultimately withdraw. This tension unaddressed has fractured the chain of knowledge transfer. The younger generation entered a world of flattened hierarchies and instant information. They respect knowledge but not necessarily rank; they question the status quo, and rightly so. Yet without spaces for guided questioning, scepticism mutates into isolation. Seniors, unsure how to bridge the divide, retreat into silence. The profession becomes a chorus of parallel monologues. Younger lawyers inhabit a different professional landscape. They are digital natives, impatient with bureaucracy, eager for results. Their sense of identity is global rather than local, and they have access to information that once took years of tutelage to obtain. Many seniors, by contrast, built their careers in an era when patience was the first proof of seriousness. To them, the new generation appears restless; to the new generation, the old appears rigid. **Both sides misread passion as arrogance and caution as fear.**This disconnect did not emerge from malice. It is the natural friction of changing times. Yet when left unaddressed, it breeds mutual suspicion. Seniors stop offering guidance because they assume it will be rejected. Juniors stop seeking guidance because they expect to be patronised. The quiet distance that follows is mentorship's silent killer.Generational tension also manifests in language. Where seniors speak of "paying dues," juniors speak of "work–life balance." Where seniors emphasise loyalty, juniors emphasise opportunity. These are not opposites; they are coordinates of the same value system—commitment balanced by fairness. But without spaces for dialogue, difference hardens into contempt. I have heard young lawyers whisper that mentorship is a disguise for exploitation; I have heard seniors mutter that the new Bar is allergic to discipline. Both are exaggerations born of fatigue.Bridging this gap requires deliberate institutional design. Intergenerational mentorship should not depend on chemistry or chance; it should be facilitated by structure. NBA branches could hold "reverse mentoring" sessions where juniors share digital strategies and seniors share courtroom judgment. Firms could pair partners with associates outside their direct teams to reduce hierarchical tension. The goal is not to erase difference but to channel it into exchange.The judiciary faces a similar challenge. Younger clerks and research assistants bring new analytical tools—data analysis, online research, comparative perspectives. Senior judges bring intuition, temperament, and procedural mastery. If each side listens, jurisprudence grows richer; if each retreat into pride, jurisprudence grows thinner. I have learned that mentoring across generations demands humility on both sides. The senior must accept that wisdom can flow upward as well as downward. The junior must understand that knowledge without context is brittle. The healthiest mentorship relationships I have witnessed are those where both sides begin with intentional curiosity and not assumption. I learned this the most during my brief but highly instructive tenure as the Director of Oaths in the F.C.T judiciary. Particularly when saddled with the herculean responsibility of pioneering a digital infrastructure in the affidavit system of the organization. This required my leveraging the three types of mentorship paradigm simultanously (upward – downward – and across)

It is soothing to know that generational disconnection is reversible, but only through proximity. No amount of online courses or motivational slogans can replace the daily, human rhythm of learning together. The Bar must therefore design environments—physical and digital—where this rhythm can thrive again.

Institutional apathy.   Institutions are meant to guard a profession's memory. When they sleep, customs fade; when they fragment, no one holds the thread of continuity. Our legal institutions—the Bar, the Bench, and the training bodies—did not deliberately abandon mentorship, but they allowed it to become optional. Over time, optionality turned into absence. Without methodical mentorship standards ingrained in our institutions, excellence becomes episodic and staggered. Institutional structures that could have preserved mentorship have remained largely passive.

However, the **Nigerian Bar Association (NBA)** has made commendable efforts—organizing mentorship fora and pairing programs—but these initiatives often lack continuity, funding, and standardized assessment. Without a clear institutional mandate that defines mentorship as an enforceable professional duty, participation remains voluntary and sporadic.

Contrast this with the **Law Society of Ontario** or the **South African Legal Practice Council**, where mentorship is built into professional certification and continuing education. In Nigeria, the **Body of Benchers**, **Council of Legal Education**, and **Law School** operate in parallel silos, each addressing legal education at different levels but none sustaining a coherent mentorship framework that bridges academia and practice

These are challenges to be managed, not excuses to be accepted.

Each of these challenges deserves its own analysis, but their cumulative effect is this: we have replaced a living culture with episodic gestures. We hold mentorship conferences, issue communiqués, and take photographs of panels; but the daily, private labour of forming another lawyer — that long conversation that stretches over months of shared work — has become rare.

The tragedy is not only professional; it is generational. Every time a senior retires without a successor shaped in both skill and ethos, the law loses more than experience — it loses memory. I had the undeniable experience of this loss few years ago as I watched, arguably, one of the most brilliant, articulate and vibrant judicial officer ever produced in the history of the federal high court of

Nigeria retire – Hon.Justice Ibrahim Buba. That day, in my opinion, the judiciary lost not just pristine experience but unmatched valuable memory.

This is exactly how Institutions forget how they once maintained standards. The next generation must start from theory rather than inheritance. That is how decline reproduces itself quietly, almost politely.

I write this not to romanticise the past but to locate the break in our continuity. If we can name the stages of the unravelling, we can design the stages of repair. Mentorship did not vanish in a day; it will not return in a day but by degree, by understanding how it slipped through our fingers, we can begin to close the gaps again.

9. Counter-Arguments—and Their Limits

Some argue that mentorship is a private process, not a public duty. I disagree. When a profession holds a monopoly over the right to represent others before courts, society has a legitimate interest in how that profession reproduces itself. **Mentorship serves as infrastructure for justice; leaving it to chance invites systemic risk.**

Others fear that formalisation will stiffen relationships. The answer is not to avoid structure, but to design light-touch frameworks bespoke enough to protect flexibility while ensuring accountability. **Freedom and standards are not adversaries; they are partners in excellence.**

10. The Nigerian Moment: What We Can Draw from Elsewhere

1. From the UK we learn the value of regulated apprenticeship.

2. From Canada, the power of linking mentorship to continuing professional development.

3. From South Africa, the possibility of integrating mentorship into judicial and public-interest training with cultural resonance.

4. From Kenya, the lesson that clear, national guidelines can lift practice across regions.

For Nigeria, the path is to translate these insights into our institutional constructs: NBA branches, the Body of Benchers, the Council of Legal Education, the National Judicial Institute, and law faculties. **We already have the architecture. What we require is alignment**.

11. Defining Mentorship for Policy (A Working Description)

For the purposes of this book and the framework proposed in later chapters, it is imperative to adopt a working definition:

> **Mentorship is a structured professional relationship, time-bound and goal-oriented, in which a more experienced legal practitioner invests knowledge, judgment, and ethical example in a less experienced lawyer, under agreed standards, with outcomes observable by the profession.**

This definition respects relationships while making space for monitoring and support.

12. The Mentor's Duties (As I Have Practiced and Observed)

A mentor should:

- **Model integrity.** Example is the loudest lecture.

- **Teach the craft.** Writing, analysis, advocacy, client care— each must be explicit, not assumed.

- **Give feedback.** Specific, prompt, and fair corrections build competence without breaking confidence.

- **Open doors responsibly.** Introduce, recommend, and then supervise.

- **Document growth.** Keeping records prevent drift and enable reflection.

The mentor's reward is twofold: **a better Bar today and a more trustworthy legacy tomorrow.**

13. The Mentee's Duties (The Apprenticeship Ethic)

A mentee should:

- **Prepare.** Do the reading before the meeting.

- **Ask precise questions.** Curiosity with discipline accelerates growth.

- **Receive correction with maturity.** Feedback is a gift; use it.

- **Protect trust.** Confidentiality is non-negotiable.

- **Pay it forward.** The chain only endures if the **formed become formers and the trainee becomes trainers**

Mentorship is not patronage. It is apprenticeship under honour.

14. The Hidden Equity Question – Mentorship, the tool of equality

Without structure, access gravitates to the already connected—major cities, elite firms, familiar networks. Women, lawyers with disabilities, and colleagues from less privileged backgrounds often face thinner pipelines. **Mentorship is therefore an equity tool.** Having a national mentorship architecture corrects this bias by widening the gate and lighting the path.

Equity is not a charity; it is a necessity that brings in a broader talent base. This inevitably strengthens the whole profession.

15. What "Institutionalising" Should—and Should Not—Mean

Should mean: clear standards, protected time, recognised contributions (e.g. award of continuous professional development -CPD- credits), light documentation, and real accountability.

Should not mean: rigid pairing of people with no chemistry, paperwork without purpose, or one-size-fits-all timelines. **The essence lies in setting a floor, not a ceiling**.

Later chapters propose a i) National Mentorship Council, ii) a Mentorship Charter, ii) accreditation for mentors, and iv) incentives - that make mentorship participation rational as well as moral.

16. Mentorship in the Judiciary: Formal Judicial Mentorship

Adjudication is not merely deciding; it is deciding well. Reasoned restraint, clarity, and moderately proportioned are habits learned in community. Formal judicial mentorship—senior judge to newly appointed judge, - converts institutional memory into living method. It is worthy of note that the judiciary at some minimal level entrenches this method by providing for formal attachments of newly appointed Judges to senior more accomplished judges immediately upon appointment. However, the National Judicial Institute as well may seek to house such programs. Our jurisprudence will be the richer for it.

17. Academia's Role: From Supervision to Formation

Universities and the Nigerian Law School shape minds at their most malleable stage. The shift we require is from supervision only (scripts, theses) to formation (ethics, professional identity, public service).

Externships, if tightly mentored and monitored, become laboratories where law meets life. Criteria that reward mentorship work—alongside research—would align incentives with outcomes.

18. Law Firms as Engines of Formation

The chambers are the workshop of the legal profession. Firms that embed mentorship into workflow—draft reviews, shadowing, structured rotations, quarterly growth meetings— produce juniors who are confident, careful, and court-ready. Smaller firms can collaborate through NBA branches to share mentors and training. Excellence must not be the monopoly of the largest firms only.

19. The Cost of Neglect (What We Already Pay)

When mentorship is thin, we pay in three currencies:

- **Ethical lapses.**
- **Skill gaps.**
- **Public trust loss.**

Interestingly it is the justice system that bears the reputational cost of our private omissions. Prevention is cheaper than repair. Mentorship is prevention.

20. A Personal Word: What My Mentors Gave Me

I was not made by the applause of men or by appointment into certain offices. I was formed and still being formed by seniors who corrected my drafts, asked me to rethink an argument, and occasionally insisted on the most ethical strategy. They showed me that courage in law is not loudness but fidelity to principle even when it is inconvenient. This book is, in part, repayment.

21. Principles to Carry Forward (A Compact of First Principles)

Before we proceed to diagnosis and design in later chapters, I set down six principles that will anchor the blueprint:

1. **Mentorship is a public trust.** The public interest justifies professional standards around it.

2. **Structure protects relationships.** Light frameworks prevent drift and abuse.

3. **Incentives matter.** Recognition and CPD alignment turn good intentions into habits.

4. **Equity strengthens excellence.** Wider access creates a level playing field, elevates the average and reveals the exceptional.

5. **Continuity is the goal.** Link law school, law practice, judiciary, and academia in one mentorship continuum.

6. **Modeling is doctrine.** No policy survives in the face of poor modelling.

22. Not Nostalgia—But Architecture

This chapter is **not a plea to return to a smaller Bar but a call to design a stronger Bar.** The spirit of mentorship we once enjoyed in fragments must now be given a home in crafted policy. If we succeed, juniors will be guided, seniors will be honoured, and the public will be better served. If we fail, we will continue to produce cleverness without compass—a loss the justice system cannot afford.

The next chapter examines how mentorship declined: the economic, cultural, technological, and institutional currents that quietly redirected our habits. **Diagnosis precedes prescription. Reform begins with facing the truth.**

CHAPTER TWO

Institutional Paradox — the Need for a National Mentorship Council.

All of these aforementioned fragments of decline add up to an institutional paradox: every stakeholder acknowledges mentorship as vital, yet none claims ownership of it. The result is duplication at best and neglect at worst. When responsibility is shared by all, it is executed by none.

I have seen this apathy expressed most clearly in budgeting. When an institution values an idea, it funds it. Mentorship rarely features as a budget line in annual plans. There are allocations for training, travel, and conferences—but rarely for the structured mentorship pairing, monitoring, or evaluation that mentorship requires. We keep talking about mentorship as though it were costless, forgetting that time is money and that systems cost something to sustain.

This decline also manifests in the chain of communication. Law faculties operate in one silo, the Law School in another, the NBA in a third, the Bench in a fourth. Each produces capable lawyers at its level, but the handoffs are clumsy. No sustainable handrails are built to co-join these silos.

A student mentored in university loses contact upon call; a young practitioner mentored in practice finds no bridge into judicial service or academia. The result is a mentorship landscape full of beginnings but few continuities.

The **Judiciary**, for its part, has relied on tradition rather than design. A few judges consciously train younger judges, explaining reasoning, style, and ethics; (I have been a fortunate beneficiary of this professional kindness) many others, pressed by caseloads omit on this responsibility.

The **National Judicial Institute** conducts excellent seminars, but a seminar is not mentorship; it is information without observation. Without sustained engagement, the human transmission of temperament and reasoning fades.

To repair this, institutions must agree on shared responsibility. The Bar should coordinate; the Bench should model; the Academy should seed. A national **Mentorship Council**, jointly owned by these bodies, would not replace individual effort but would align it. Coordination does not stifle creativity—it channels it. When everyone pulls in rhythm, even small strokes move the canoe faster.

Institutional apathy is not about bad people; it is about busy people, too busy to pay attention. Each segment of the profession is consumed with its own urgent tasks—litigation backlogs, administrative reforms, curriculum reviews. Yet mentorship is the quiet infrastructure that holds these tasks together. Without it, efficiency reforms become mechanical. If we wish for a stronger profession, we must weave mentorship into the mandates of every governing body.

Technology and the Vanishing Chambers

As previously discussed, technology has changed how we work, how we learn, and even how we relate. I am among those who welcome this change and in fact at some time, pioneered same: digital filing, online research, virtual hearings—these have made the law faster, broader, and more accessible. Yet I have also watched something precious slip through the cracks: the informal apprenticeship that once grew naturally from proximity. The chambers, in its physical sense, has begun to vanish.

When I was a young lawyer practicing in Ibadan Oyo state in the chambers of L.O Fagbemi SAN & Co, the chambers was a school disguised as an office. We read in one another's presence; we listened as seniors dictated and argued; we followed them to court, observing tone, posture, and courtesy. Mistakes were corrected in real time; the day ended with quiet debriefs over case law. That environment taught more than the law—it taught the rhythm of the profession.

Now, much of this rhythm occurs in silence. Drafts move through email threads; meetings migrate to online platforms. Juniors can work for months without sitting across from their supervisors. Feedback is brief, transactional, and often delayed. In this new efficiency, the incidental lessons—the way a senior greets a judge, negotiates a settlement, or handles a difficult client—rarely reach the next generation. **We have gained speed but lost texture**.

The digital revolution has also changed where young lawyers work. Remote and hybrid arrangements, while convenient, fragment the collective experience of learning together. As mentioned in chapter one, Mentorship requires observation, not only instruction. One learns by being near—by hearing, by seeing, by absorbing the unscripted. When proximity disappears, tacit knowledge evaporates. The legal profession thrives on nuance; technology transmits data, not nuance.

This is not an argument against progress. It is a call to redesign progress with human contact intact. **We can use technology to enhance mentorship rather than replace it.** Virtual platforms can host structured mentorship sessions, allowing juniors in remote regions to connect with experienced mentors across the country. Online collaboration tools can document feedback transparently. The key is intentionality: if we do not consciously embed mentorship into our digital workflows, the algorithm will quietly decide what matters—and it will not choose mentorship.

I have read and heard of encouraging models abroad. In Canada, the Law Society of Ontario maintains an online mentorship portal where pairings are algorithmically matched but humanly sustained. In Kenya, the Council of Legal Education uses digital logs for pupillage reporting, ensuring accountability without removing personal contact. Nigeria can adopt similar hybrids.

But we must also protect physical mentorship spaces. Law firms and government agencies should design their offices not only for productivity but for presence. Senior lawyers need offices that open outward, not upward—spaces where juniors can observe and learn. The Law School and Bar Centers must revive the idea of study circles, where experience is exchanged rather than broadcasted.

Technology promises connection but its danger is isolation. If we allow the screens to mediate every conversation, we risk producing lawyers fluent in information but foreign to judgment and discernment. Mentorship is still, at its core, a human encounter. **Our task is not to resist technology or innovation but to humanize it—to make sure that in digitalizing the law, we do not delete its soul.**

Enthusiasm is a Lone Voice

Every time I meet newly called counsel or a young lawyer, I am reminded that enthusiasm alone cannot sustain a career. The moral fire of a young advocate quickly dims when rent is due, salaries lag, and the profession's promises feel abstract. It is easy to speak of discipline and patience from a stable perch; it is harder to hear those virtues when one cannot afford transportation to court. **Economic hardship has become a silent saboteur of mentorship.**

Many juniors today enter practice with loans or family obligations. The first few years, which should be a season of learning, turn into a season of survival. They drift between poorly paid clerkships, chasing briefs that barely cover appearance fees. Some abandon practice altogether, seeking refuge in corporate employment, compliance work, or politics. I do not condemn them; the system gives them little choice. My early experience was in the similitude of this as well. But each departure of these new wigs drains the Bar of future mentors.

Low remuneration also distorts the mentoring relationship itself. When a junior's livelihood depends entirely on the goodwill of a senior, guidance can blur into dependency. **The healthiest mentorships are those grounded in respect, not rescue.** Yet in many firms, young lawyers become errand runners— overworked, underpaid, and too intimidated to complain. These dynamic breeds resentment on one side and defensiveness on the other. Instead of forming character, it deforms it.

I recall one conversation with a brilliant young lawyer who confided that he had learned to "self-mentor" through online materials because his principal had no time to teach. "My Lord," he said, "I just watch recordings of court sessions online and guess what judges naturally prefer." His ingenuity impressed me, but his loneliness troubled me. The law is not meant to be learned in isolation. Self-study produces competence; supervision produces judgment and discernment.

The Bar must therefore treat young-lawyer's welfare as a structural issue, not a charitable gesture. Fair stipends, transparent employment contracts, and minimum standards for chambers remuneration are not luxuries; they are mentorship enablers. Without economic stability, no amount of rhetoric will create teachable minds. **Hunger breeds' haste; haste erodes ethics.**

Several reforms are within reach. Branches of the Nigerian Bar Association could maintain verified employment rosters and publish annual surveys of remuneration ranges to encourage transparency. Law firms that meet fair-pay and mentorship standards could earn public recognition, perhaps through something like - an NBA "Mentorship-Friendly Firm" certification. To think of it, corporate clients might prefer to brief firms with that kind of a label, linking market reputation to ethical practice.

Public institutions also have a role. The Legal Aid Council, Ministry of Justice, and state judiciaries employ hundreds of young lawyers. If each built structured mentorship tracks—pairing recruits with seasoned counsel, rotating assignments, reviewing progress quarterly—we would convert entry-level employment into professional formation. The cost is modest and the return is immense.

Finally, we must address the psychological toll. The profession should normalise mentorship that includes emotional guidance—how to handle failure, criticism, and fatigue. The image of the tireless lawyer who never falters is a myth; even the strong need reassurance. True mentorship acknowledges this humanity.

If we fail to address the socio-economic strain on our youngest members, we risk producing a generation technically qualified but disengaged from the spirit of the profession—lawyers who know the rules but no longer believe in the calling. Restoring mentorship therefore begins with restoring dignity. Dignity has a cost, but neglect costs more.

Ethical and Competence Consequences

When mentorship weakens, the damage does not announce itself with headlines; it seeps quietly into the bloodstream of the profession. I see it in small lapses that multiply over time—**careless filings by lawyers that creates untoward back lash on Judges work**, disrespectful correspondence, arguments without substance, and a growing confusion between cleverness and integrity. Ethics and competence, once reinforced by daily modelling, begin to drift apart.

1. The Erosion of Professional Courtesy

Professional courtesy is the first casualty. The young lawyer who has never seen a senior apologise to a court will not easily learn humility. In the absence of modelling, assertiveness degenerates into aggressiveness. Judges experience this as rudeness; clients mistake it for confidence; colleagues call it "the new style." Courtesy may not be a rule—but it is a habit learned by watching restraint exercised under pressure. **Where mentorship fails, manners follow.**

2. Ethical Confusion

Next comes ethical confusion. Many young lawyers genuinely wish to act correctly but are uncertain where the lines lie. The Rules of Professional Conduct (2023) give guidance, yet their interpretation demands context. For example, how far may one press a procedural advantage before it becomes abuse of process? When does persuasion become misrepresentation? These questions are best answered through example and modeling, not lectures. Without seniors demonstrating discernment, young practitioners are left to guess—and these guesses are sometimes costly.

3. Competence Without a Sence of Judgment

I have encountered lawyers who are technically adept—fluent in digital research, persuasive in writing and speech—yet lacking the delicate balance of judgment. They can find their authorities but not their priorities. They win interlocutory skirmishes and lose the client's war. This is not a failure of intellect but of formation. Judgment matures through guided exposure to consequence: seeing how a senior weighs not only what can be done but what should be done. Without such formation, brilliance becomes brittle over time.

4. The Shortcut Culture

Mentorship decay also feeds a shortcut culture. When young lawyers see success measured only by outcomes, not by method, they begin to value victory over virtue. Copying precedents without comprehension, undercutting colleagues, or courting clients through unethical means—these are symptoms of an ecosystem where guidance is absent. The profession's collective reputation then pays the price. Each disciplinary case we read in the news is not only an individual's failure; it is the echo of a missing mentor.

5. The Public Trust Deficit

Public trust, once lost, is hardest to regain. The ordinary citizen cannot assess a lawyer's technical ability on the face of it, but they can sense integrity. When court processes become combative and correspondence uncivil, the lay man observer perceives a trade, not a vocation. Mentorship is the unseen infrastructure that sustains public faith in legal decorum. Without it, we may still produce advocates, but fewer officers of justice.

6. The Judicial Ripple

The consequences extend to the Bench as well. A poorly mentored Bar eventually produces a fragile Bench. Judges emerge from the same pool of practitioners they once were. The mentorship that fails in chambers, eventually enters into the courtrooms. The same gaps in discipline, writing, and empathy that we tolerate today become systemic tomorrow. The chain is continuous.

7. Institutional Cost

Ethical lapses also carry institutional cost. Bar disciplinary committees, once rarely convened, now operate in near permanence. Firms expend resources on damage control; courts lose time on frivolous applications and **applications fraught with senseless irregularities aimed at setting vain traps for the judicial officer**. All these are the loud echoes of mentorship gaps. Training budgets grow but formation shrinks. The cure is never as efficient as prevention.

To restore ethics and competence, we must treat mentorship as the first line of professional regulation. Rules can instruct; but mentors help internalise. Sanctions can deter; but it is mentors who transforms. A profession that relies solely on punishment to enforce ethics has already surrendered its moral authority. What we need is a culture where good conduct is not enforced but expected—because it has been witnessed.

Mentorship Neglect: A Policy Problem.

The neglect of mentorship has become a policy problem as much as a cultural one. - (a policy problem is a social issue that now requires structural or governmental intervention to provide a solution). The profession presently lives with the compound interest of decades of neglect. Every reform conversation begins from deficit. **If we can quantify its cost, perhaps we will stop treating it as sentimental nostalgia and start treating it as strategic necessity**.

1. The Hidden Economics of Poor Formation

When mentorship declines, inefficiency rises. Juniors spend longer on tasks they could have mastered sooner; seniors lose billable hours correcting preventable errors; clients pay twice for the same learning curve. The aggregate economic cost is significant, though invisible in ledgers. In public service, the impact is harsher: delayed prosecutions, inconsistent drafting, poorly reasoned opinions. These are not isolated blunders; they are the predictable outcomes of under-mentored systems.

2. The Governance Cost

Weak mentorship corrodes institutional continuity. Each new Bar leadership must "start afresh," unaware of what was attempted before. Courts reinvent administrative practices already tested elsewhere. Law faculties struggle to maintain consistent quality as seasoned lecturers retire without successors ready to assume the baton. Governance becomes cyclical rather than progressive.

3. The Ethical Cost

Disciplinary processes expand in proportion to the mentorship deficit. The Bar spends time policing conduct that could have been prevented through guidance. Judges deliver rebukes that could have been unnecessary had advocacy been shaped earlier. An ethics regime that relies entirely on sanctions rather than formation ends up reactive and weary. The human cost—public shame, lost careers, diminished faith in justice—cannot be measured but can be prevented.

4. The Social Cost

The public looks to lawyers for more than representation; it looks for reassurance that justice is being tended by people of discipline and conscience. Each instance of misconduct reverberates beyond the individuals involved—it erodes the moral authority of the entire legal system. The Bar's failure to mentor its young is, ultimately, a failure owed to society.

5. The Emotional Cost

I have spoken several times with young lawyers who confess to feeling adrift—unsure of their path, unseen by seniors, unanchored in purpose. This quiet despair rarely makes the news, but it seeps into work and life. **Disengagement is the prelude to departure**, whether to other professions or to cynicism within this one. Mentorship, when present, offers belonging; when its absent, it breeds isolation.

6. What the Data Suggests

Emerging research from legal education studies underscores the link between structured mentorship and performance. Jurisdictions with formal mentorship programs report lower disciplinary issues and higher retention of women and minorities in practice. The numbers confirm what experience already teaches: **formation is more efficient than correction.**

7. From Sentiment to Strategy

The answer is not nostalgia but architecture. Mentorship must be planned, funded, and evaluated like any other aspect of professional development. NBA branches should incorporate it into annual performance metrics; it should be treated as a criterion for renewal of practicing license or even accreditation where required; the Judiciary should embed it within judicial training modules. **Mentorship is not charity—it is necessity.**

8. The Cost of Inaction

If we continue on the current path, the legal profession will produce increasing numbers of technically competent but ethically fragile lawyers. The ripple effects will reach the courts, the economy, and the credibility of governance itself. When citizens lose faith in those who interpret the law, they begin to doubt the law itself. That is the ultimate cost of neglect.

Counting the Cost to Inspire Change

Mentorship is not the solution to every professional challenge, but without it, no solution endures. The economics of practice, the gaps in ethics, the widening distance between law school and court—all trace back to the same root: formation without guidance. We have measured the loss; in the next chapter, we will look outward to see how other jurisdictions have turned similar losses into renewal. Their stories prove that decline is not destiny.

CHAPTER THREE

Comparative Jurisprudence — Lessons from Global Mentorship Systems

The Purpose of Comparative Study

When a profession begins to lose its way, wisdom often lies in looking sideways rather than backward. Other Commonwealth jurisdictions have wrestled with the same questions that now

confront us: How can mentorship be scaled without killing spontaneity? How can we honour tradition while meeting the demands of modern practice? studying these systems is not with the aim to copy them but to distil principles adaptable to our own terrain.

The kinship of common law gives us a shared vocabulary. What differs is the strategy of implementation—the policy choices that we make.

Across the United Kingdom, Canada, South Africa, Kenya, and Australia, in my studies, I found one common insight: mentorship flourishes when responsibility is clearly assigned, performance is measured, and culture is reinforced by incentives. The rest of this chapter explores how each jurisdiction translated that insight into practice.

United Kingdom — Structure as Custodian

The English Bar built mentorship into its bloodstream through the **Inns of Court**. Pupillage remains a prerequisite for call; it lasts one year and is governed by the **Bar Standards Board (BSB)**. - "The Bar Standards Board regulates barristers and specialised legal services businesses in England and Wales in the public interest."- Each pupil is paired with a pupil-supervisor, who must be accredited and periodically reviewed. The supervisor is not a benevolent volunteer but a regulated participant in professional reproduction construct.

I have never visited the Inner Temple before but the accounts of those who have, reports that what is most striking about the inner Temple is not grandeur but system. Each Inn maintains records of mentorship sessions, requires written feedback, and subjects supervisors to oversight. Pupils attend ethics courses and advocacy workshops built into the mentorship cycle. In this way, tradition and modern accountability coexist.

I believe that for Nigeria, the British example offers a procedural template rather than a cultural one. We need not replicate the Inns; but we can replicate their insistence that mentoring is an enforceable duty. Where standards exist, culture follows.

Canada — Mentorship as Continuing Development

Canada's model extends mentorship beyond the entry phase. The **Law Society of Ontario** requires every articling student to work under a principal—a senior lawyer approved by the society. But Canada went further: many provinces now integrate mentorship into **Continuing Professional Development (CPD)**. A lawyer who mentors earns CPD credits equal to those earned by attending seminars. - (An articling student in Canada is a law graduate undergoing a supervised, full-time, practical training period required to become a licensed lawyer. This apprenticeship, often called "articles," is a mandatory step where students gain hands-on experience in a law firm or other legal setting under the guidance of an approved principal.) -

I admire the elegance of the CPD solution. It aligns virtue with incentive; it makes guidance economically rational. In Alberta and British Columbia, bar associations also operate voluntary mentorship networks linking lawyers across practice areas and generations, both online and in person. The systems are supported by staff, budgets, and data—proof that goodwill alone is not the strategy that gets things done. You need budget, you need staffing and credible data.

For Nigeria, this linkage between mentorship and CPD could transform participation from sporadic to steady. If teaching earns as much credit as listening, more seniors will teach.

South Africa — Mentorship as Transformation

South Africa faced a dual challenge: rebuilding its legal institutions after apartheid while widening access for historically excluded groups. The **Legal Practice Act 28 of 2014** confronted both by embedding mentorship within transformation. Candidate attorneys must serve under approved principals, and the **Legal**

Practice Council (LPC) audits compliance. The program emphasises not only skill but social responsibility; community-based law clinics and pro bono mentorship count toward completion.

During my online research into South African legal practice system, I came across a phrase that intrigued me: "Ubuntu chambers." It describes offices where seniors view guidance as communal duty, not private charity. The South African experience shows that mentorship can be both regulatory and cultural. Nigeria's diversity demands a similar moral imagination: mentorship not just to preserve excellence, but to equalise opportunity.

Kenya — The Rise of Structured Pupillage

The **Law Society of Kenya (LSK)** and the **Council of Legal Education** jointly regulate pupillage under clear guidelines issued in 2019. Mentors must sign training plans; mentees maintain logs assessed by supervisors and validated by the LSK. Even small firms participate through cluster mentorship—several seniors pooling resources to train groups of pupils.

Kenya's success lies in collaboration. The LSK, the judiciary, and the academia share a common database, preventing the fragmentation that hinders Nigeria. They treat mentorship data as governance data. That integration is precisely what our institutions need: coordination rather than competition.

Australia — From Goodwill to Governance

Australia's state bar associations transformed mentorship from informal courtesy to administrative requirement. In Victoria and New South Wales, every new barrister must complete a supervised practice program, and failure to report progress delays full admission. The supervising barrister's obligation is documented; breaches invite inquiry. Yet the system remains humane: **mentors are supported through workshops and recognition awards**.

I am honestly intrigued by their reward system. The Australians discovered that **regulation without appreciation breeds compliance, not commitment.** They therefore celebrate mentors publicly, publishing success stories and best-practice guides. And this reminds the profession and the world that **mentorship is an honourable work, not a bureaucratic burden**.

Shared Lessons for Nigeria

Across these Commonwealth examples, five lessons recur:

1. **Regulate lightly but clearly.** Standards can protect relationships without suffocating them.

2. **Reward participation.** Link mentorship to CPD, appointment eligibility, and public recognition preferably organized at NBA award nights during the annual general conferences

3. **Record progress.** Data ensures continuity across leadership changes. It helps leadership remain a continuum.

4. **Integrate institutions.** Bar, Bench, and Academia must share responsibility and share information.

5. **Connect mentorship to justice.** Directly link mentorship to the quality of justice dispensed. The ultimate measure is not the number of pairings but the quality of advocates and judges produced.

These jurisdictions prove that **mentorship can be formal without being mechanical**. The secret lies in design that respects both accountability and autonomy.

Comparative Wisdom, Local Application

Each nation translated its history into its mentoring architecture. The United Kingdom formalised tradition; Canada incentivised it; South Africa moralised it; Kenya coordinated it; Australia normalised it. Our task is to contextualise it. Nigeria's profession is too vast and too vital for neglect. We can borrow the bones of these systems but must clothe them in our own cultural fabric.

As I studied these models, one conviction grew clearer: mentorship thrives where the profession agrees that forming others is part of practising well. That agreement is what Chapter Four will seek to test within our borders. How does the Nigerian legal profession now train its own? Where does mentorship still live, and where has it fallen silent?

CHAPTER FOUR

The Nigerian Legal Profession — Mapping the Mentorship Landscape

Introduction — Many Parents, few Guardians.

Each time I attend or even speak at a call-to-bar ceremony, I am struck by how many institutions shape the same lawyer: the university, the Law School, the Bar, the Bench, the Ministry of Justice etc. We are a profession with many parents but few guardians. Mentorship lives within all these bodies, yet none holds full custody. To institutionalise mentorship, we must first understand where it already exists and where it has faded.

The Council of Legal Education and the Nigerian Law School

The Legal Education (Consolidation, etc.) Act establishes the **Council of Legal Education** (CLE) to regulate professional training and to maintain the **Nigerian Law School**. The CLE's mandate includes the "training of persons to be called to the Bar," but not the ongoing mentorship of those already called. The Law School therefore performs the first, but not the full, act of formation.

Mentorship at this level occurs mainly through teaching conferences, externships, and ethics classes. The compulsory Law Office and Court Attachment Programme is the school's closest approximation of structured mentorship. In theory, every student is placed under a practising lawyer or judge; in practice, the quality varies widely. Some hosts invest time in teaching; others provide little more than a desk while some hosts do not even engage them at all.

The solution is refinement, not reinvention. The CLE could:

- accredit law offices specifically as mentorship chambers, with periodic evaluation;

- issue a national externship handbook defining objectives and assessment methods;

- introduce a post-attachment or a pre-attachment reflection paper linking classroom theory to field experience.

Such modest steps would shift the externship from just exposure to real formation and identity crafting.

The Nigerian Bar Association (NBA)

The **NBA**, the profession's umbrella body, is the most natural custodian of mentorship. Its constitution (as amended 2022) lists among its aims "the maintenance and advancement of legal education and professional conduct." Several initiatives already exist—the **Young Lawyers Forum (YLF)**, branch mentorship committees, and the annual **NBA Mentorship Programme** at the national conference. The difficulty lies in continuity.

Each administration tends to start anew; databases disappear, budgets lapse, and reporting is uneven. To be honest, branches in Lagos, Abuja, and Port Harcourt have done better, running structured pairing systems with defined tenure and evaluation. Smaller branches, constrained by resources, rely on ad-hoc goodwill.

Three reforms in my opinion, can move the NBA from rhetoric to routine:

1. **National Mentorship Registry** — a digital platform where mentors and mentees register, log meetings, and receive CPD points.

2. **Standard Operating Guidelines** — a short document prescribing expectations and confidentiality rules.

3. **Annual Mentorship Audit** — each branch to report progress annually as a standard mandatory requirement .

If the NBA links mentorship participation to leadership eligibility and award recognition, the culture will root itself within five years.

The Judiciary — Custodian of Temperament

Within the **Judiciary**, mentorship is both natural and inherent. Every courtroom is a classroom; every judgment a lecture. Yet formal mentorship remains limited. The **National Judicial Institute (NJI)** provides orientation for newly appointed judges and continuing judicial education, but mentorship rarely extends beyond seminars.

A judge's greatest influence is exercised in chambers: through interaction with research assistants, registrars, and clerks.

The NJI could embed mentorship into its curriculum by:

- pairing each new judge with a senior "Judicial Guide" for the first year;

- assessing progress through reflective reports, not examinations;

- hosting quarterly peer-learning or peer- review circles on judgment writing and ethics.

Such a one year or half a year programme would require little funding but would preserve the Bench's collective culture, temperament and unique nature.

Legal Academia — Mentorship Nurseries

Universities were once nurseries of mentorship. Professors knew their students by name; tutorials were conversations, not lectures. Today, overcrowded classrooms and administrative burdens have thinned that intimacy. Academic promotion systems reward publications more than guidance, so mentorship competes with metrics.

The **Network of University Legal Aid Institutions (NULAI)** has revived clinical education across faculties, linking students with supervisors handling real cases. This model, if extended, could anchor mentorship through practice. Faculties could also:

.

- include mentorship contribution in appraisal criteria;

- establish alumni-student mentorship clubs under the guidance of lecturers;

- collaborate with the NBA for joint mentoring events.

When academia reclaims its mentoring role, the pipeline between classroom and courtroom will strengthen.

Law Firms — The Home of Mentorship

Private practice remains mentorship's most natural home. Large commercial firms in Lagos and Abuja have adopted structured associate-development programmes—rotations, writing clinics, shadowing of partners. Smaller firms rely on the apprenticeship model, but often without documentation.

The challenge here, is disparity. A young lawyer in a major firm enjoys systematic guidance; one in a provincial or local small office may receive none. The NBA could bridge this gap through cluster mentorship: several small firms pooling seniors to train their juniors collectively. Firms should also receive public recognition for excellence in mentorship—perhaps an NBA Seal of Mentorship Quality. Reputation is a powerful incentive.

Public Sector and Legal Aid Institutions

The **Federal Ministry of Justice**, **state Ministries of Justice**, and the **Legal Aid Council of Nigeria** employ thousands of young counsel. These bodies already have hierarchical supervision but rarely structured mentoring. If each department adopted a mentorship framework—pairing new officers with seniors, rotating case types, reviewing progress semi-annually—the state would become the largest training ground for ethical advocacy.

The **National Human Rights Commission** and **EFCC** could adopt similar internal mentorship constructs. Public institutions often set norms the private sector later mirrors.

Synthesis — Strengths, Gaps, and Opportunities

Across these institutions, mentorship survives but in fragments:

Sector	Strength	Gap	Opportunity
Legal Education	Nationwide coverage	Inconsistent supervision	Accreditation of mentorship chambers
NBA	Enthusiastic branches	Lack of continuity	National registry & audit

Judiciary	Deep experience	Limited structured pairing	NJI Judicial Guide Scheme
Academia	Intellectual depth	Weak student contact	Mentorship counted for promotion
Private Practice	Innovation in big firms	Rural inequality	Cluster mentorship model
Public Sector	Stable employment	No formal mentorship	Departmental mentoring frameworks

Fragmentation is curable through coordination. A **National Mentorship Council**—jointly owned by the CLE, NBA, NJI, and Body of Benchers—could weave these threads into one continuum, from classroom to courtroom to chamber to bench. Its secretariat need not be large; its authority must be clear.

From Mapping to Mobilisation

Mapping reveals both weakness and hope. The Nigerian legal profession is rich in experience but only poor in systems. The will to mentor is high; what is missing is the framework to sustain it. The next chapter proposes that framework—**how to build a national architecture where mentorship is no longer left to goodwill but guaranteed by design.**

CHAPTER FIVE

Building a Strategic Framework — Institutionalising Mentorship

From Aspiration to Architecture

For many years we have spoken of mentorship as virtue; now we must treat it as infrastructure. Goodwill built the foundation, but goodwill alone cannot sustain a system of over seventy-five thousand practising lawyers spread across a federation as vast and diverse as ours. We need an architecture—an agreed set of structures, incentives, and responsibilities that make mentorship as predictable as court sittings or continuing professional development.

Institutionalisation does not mean bureaucratisation. It means translating noble intentions into durable mechanisms. It means **designing a framework so clear that even when leadership changes, mentorship continues.** I have seen enough well-meant programmes fade because they belonged to personalities rather than to policy. This is the beauty of creating structures and systems which make for continuity and durability. The aim of this chapter is to ensure that the mentorship culture no longer depends on who happens to care, but on what the profession has agreed to care about and require.

In developing this blueprint, I am guided by three convictions drawn from both comparative study done and my experiences as a young practicing lawyer 23 years ago, to being a lower court judex for 18 years, then pioneering a major digital shift in the judiciary as a Director of oaths and now as a judge. The three convictions are that;

1. **Structure protects spirit.** When expectations are written down or codified, good relationships flourish instead of fading.

2. **Incentives sustain ideals.** People repeat what is rewarded, not merely what is requested.

3. **Accountability preserves continuity.** Measurement may feel clinical and sometimes unwieldy, but it is the only guarantee for vision to outlive the visionary.

The proposals that follow are not theoretical. They draw from conversations with colleagues in the Federal High Court, the Nigerian Bar Association, the Law School students on attachment to my court over the years, and law faculties; from observing how judicial training now operates at the National Judicial Institute; and from the global examples reviewed in the previous chapter. Each recommendation is designed to be practical, resource-sensitive, and immediately adaptable.

Our goal is a National Mentorship Ecosystem—one profession, multiple entry points, shared standards. The framework rests on the seven principles of a living system:

1.Governance and regulation,

2. Integration,

3. Incentives,

4. Evaluation,

5. Inclusivity, and

6. sustainability.

Each principle answers a single question: who leads, how we measure, and how we keep the flame alive.

In the next section I'll outline the first and most crucial pillar—**Governance and Coordination**—the engine room that will ensure every other reform finds direction.

Principle One – Governance and Coordination.

If mentorship is to survive leadership cycles, it must have an institution to guard it. Every other reform—standards, incentives, training—depends on clear coordination. I therefore propose the establishment of a **National Mentorship Council (NMC)**, a small but permanent body charged with policy design, oversight, and data stewardship for the entire legal profession.

1. Mandate

The NMC's purpose would be simple: to ensure that every lawyer in Nigeria has structured access to guidance at defined stages of their practice, and that every mentor has institutional support to give young lawyers guidance and strategy. Its functions should include:

- developing and publishing national mentorship guidelines;

- accrediting mentors and approving mentorship programmes across institutions;

- maintaining a digital mentorship registry;

- monitoring and evaluating progress through annual reports;

- advising the Body of Benchers and Council of Legal Education on reforms linked to mentorship outcomes.

The Council would not replace the Nigerian Bar Association or the National Judicial Institute; it would coordinate their overlapping efforts.

2. Suggested Composition

Membership should reflect the profession's breadth and depth :

- Chairperson: a Justice of the Court of Appeal or Supreme Court (nominated by the Chief Justice of Nigeria).

- Representatives from the Nigerian Bar Association, National Judicial Institute, Council of Legal Education,

Body of Benchers, and Nigerian Law School.

- One member from legal academia nominated by the Committee of Deans of Law.

- One representative from the Attorney-General of the Federation's office.

- Two youth representatives nominated by the Young Lawyers Forum (rotating biennially).

- An Executive Secretary appointed through open process to manage day-to-day operations.

A nine-to-eleven-member structure is sufficient—lean enough for efficiency, broad enough for legitimacy.

3. Secretariat and Operations

The NMC's secretariat could be housed within the NBA's national secretariat in Abuja for proximity to the Bar's administrative machinery, but its funding should be jointly provided by the Body of Benchers, Council of Legal Education, and NBA. This joint funding symbolises shared ownership.

Key operational tools:

- **The National Mentorship Registry** – a secure digital database recording mentors, mentees, pairings, and progress reports.

- **Annual Mentorship Report** – public summary of participation, success stories, and recommendations.

- **Policy Advisory Notes** – short briefs to guide institutions based on observed trends.

A small team of analysts and administrative officers could manage the system. Technology should be deployed to replace bureaucracy.

4. Legal Foundation

The Council's legitimacy can be established without creating new law. A Memorandum of Understanding signed by the participating bodies—NBA, NJI, CLE, and Body of Benchers—can operationalise it within months. Later, its functions may be codified through amendments to the Rules of Professional Conduct (2023) or the Legal Practitioners Act. Implementation could be made precede legislation; success will justify the formalisation gap.

5. Regional Structure

To prevent Abuja-centrism, each geopolitical zone should host a Zonal Mentorship Desk within the NBA's regional structures. These desks will:

- collect data;

- coordinate branch programmes;

- mediate between mentors and mentees in the zone.

A National Council without regional presence would become remote; decentralisation makes the policy more visible.

6. Reporting and Transparency

Every year the NMC should publish a concise State of Mentorship Report. This document—three pages of data and three of reflection—would highlight participation rates, gender balance, and identified challenges. It will make mentorship measurable and public, ensuring that promises translate into progress.

7. Culture of Collaboration

Most importantly, the NMC must embody collaboration rather than control. Its authority will derive from credibility, not coercion. When the Bar, Bench, and Academy see that data and coordination improve their own mandates, cooperation will follow naturally. Governance in this sense is not domination; it is alignment.

Principle Two – Regulation and Standards

Governance gives direction; regulation gives shape. A mentorship system without clear standards soon collapses into good intentions. When every mentor knows what is expected and every mentee knows what to demand, the relationship gains dignity and protection.

1. The Mentorship Charter

The first instrument of regulation should be a concise Mentorship Charter—six to eight clauses capturing the ethics and obligations of both sides. It should cover confidentiality, respect, time commitment, conflict of interest, and non-discrimination. The Charter must be signed before a pairing begins, just as advocates sign an oath to the court. By writing the duties down, we make them real.

2. Accreditation of Mentors

Mentors should be accredited by the **National Mentorship Council (NMC)** after meeting minimum criteria:

- at least ten years post-call experience;

- clean disciplinary record;

- demonstrable commitment to continuing professional development;

- willingness to submit periodic progress summaries.

Accreditation is not elitism; it is assurance. It protects young lawyers from unfit guides and shields mentors from unfounded complaints and unreasonable requests or expectations. Accreditation should be renewed every three years through brief refresher workshops—light touch.

3. Scope of Engagement

The NMC should define three tiers of mentorship:

1. **Entry Level (0–3 years post-call)** – focus on practical competence and ethics.

2. **Intermediate (4–9 years)** – focus on specialisation and leadership skills.

3. **Advanced (10 years and above)** – peer mentorship and succession planning.

Each tier will have tailored objectives and suggested duration, ensuring mentorship is a continuum rather than a single rite of passage.

4. Time and Documentation Standards

A mentorship cycle should run six to twelve months, with at least one documented meeting every month. Mentees should keep a simple Learning Log; mentors should record a one-page summary at the end. Forms can be digital to minimise paperwork. Documentation is not bureaucracy—it is memory and records.

5. Quality Assurance and Ethical Oversight

Complaints of neglect, exploitation, or bias must be heard swiftly. Each NBA branch should maintain a Mentorship Ethics Sub-Committee empowered to mediate disputes and, where necessary, suspend accreditation. **Transparency sustains trust**.

6. Integration with Professional Conduct

To anchor the Charter in law, a new **Rule 15A of the Rules of Professional Conduct (2023)** could read:

> "A legal practitioner of ten years standing or more shall, where circumstances permit, mentor one or more junior practitioners in accordance with guidelines issued by the Nigerian Bar Association; and failure to do so without reasonable cause may be considered conduct unbecoming of a legal practitioner."

Such a rule would signal that mentorship is a professional duty, not optional benevolence.

7. Recognition and Renewal

Accredited mentors should be publicly recognized and remarkably dedicated mentors should be publicly celebrated—at Bar conferences, in NBA bulletins, and on NBA websites. Recognition strengthens compliance more effectively than reprimand. A mentor whose name appears on the national roll will guard that honour with pride.

8. A Living Pipeline

Imagine a young woman entering university with interest in advocacy. She joins a faculty mentorship cell guided by a lecturer who encourages her to specialise in human rights. During her Law School attachment, she is placed under an accredited mentor at a public-interest firm. Upon call, her NBA branch pairs her with a senior advocate who hones her courtroom craft. Years later, as she joins the Bench, the NJI assigns her a judicial guide to refine temperament. At each stage, records, evaluations, and continuity exist. This is the vision of integration—a profession that raises its own.

Principle Three – Integration Across Institutions

Mentorship withers when it lives in silos. For decades, the legal profession's components have acted like parallel courts: each claiming jurisdiction over a phase of a lawyer's life, none exercising continuity. To institutionalise mentorship, we must connect these fragments into a single continuum—education, admission, practice, and adjudication flowing into one another.

1. The Continuum Model

This can be pictured as a river. **The universities** are the source, **the Law School** is the confluence, **the Bar** is the main current, and **the Bench** is the delta that spreads wisdom outward. If mentorship dries up at any point, the entire river loses depth. The framework therefore must design formal linkages at each stage.

2. Universities and Law Faculties

At the academic level, mentorship should begin as intellectual apprenticeship. Faculties can:

- Establish **Mentorship Cells**—small student groups attached to senior lecturers or alumni volunteers.

- Partner with local NBA branches for periodic "Classroom to Courtroom" clinics.

- Count mentorship activity in staff appraisals to reward teachers who invest in students beyond lectures.

These steps cost little but build continuity between the scholar and the practitioner.

3. The Nigerian Law School

The Law School's externship is already the closest thing to formal mentorship; it must simply be professionalised. The **Council of Legal Education** and the **NMC** could jointly issue a national Mentorship Handbook setting objectives for supervisors, assessment templates, and reporting formats. Supervising lawyers and judges would earn CPD points for effective guidance. The School, in return, would gather feedback from students to improve placements. Mentorship would thus become an evaluated component of the Bar Finals programme.

4. The Nigerian Bar Association

Within practice, the **NBA** remains the profession's heartbeat. Its branches should operationalise mentorship through **Mentorship Liaison Officers**, responsible for pairing, progress tracking, and branch reports. Every lawyer called within the past five years should automatically be enrolled in a mentorship cycle. Every accredited mentor should report to the branch liaison, who compiles data for the National Mentorship Council.

Cross-institutional events—joint workshops between judges and advocates, or "Bar–Bench Mentorship Forums"—would restore a sense of shared purpose that goes beyond litigation.

5. The Judiciary

The **National Judicial Institute (NJI)** can align its training programmes with mentorship principles. Newly appointed judges could undergo a one-year Guided Service under a senior judicial officer. Clerks and research assistants should be formally trained through mentorship modules that emphasise ethics and judgment writing. The NJI's periodic seminars can include mentor–mentee dialogues, turning abstract ethics into lived examples.

Such judicial mentorship preserves temperament—the hardest quality to teach, yet the most vital for justice.

6. Academia and the Profession

Law faculties should not end their relationship with graduates at call. Through alumni networks and continuing education partnerships, universities can remain part of the mentorship ecosystem. Professors could serve as mentors on research ethics, legal writing, and public-interest law. This collaboration between academia and the practising Bar deepens both.

7. Coordination through the National Mentorship Council

The National Mentorship Council functions as the conductor of this orchestra. It ensures that data flows smoothly across institutions: the Law School reports externship outcomes to the NBA; the NBA shares mentorship participation rates with the

NJI; the NJI informs the Body of Benchers of judicial mentorship results. In this way, mentorship becomes an unbroken thread from student to jurist.

8. A Living Pipeline

Imagine a young woman entering university with interest in advocacy. She joins a faculty mentorship cell guided by a lecturer who encourages her to specialise in human rights. During her Law School attachment, she is placed under an accredited mentor at a public-interest firm. Upon call, her NBA branch pairs her with a senior advocate who hones her courtroom craft. Years later, as she joins the Bench, the NJI assigns her a judicial guide to refine temperament. At each stage, records, evaluations, and continuity exist. This is the vision of integration—a profession that raises its own.

Principle Four – Incentives and Recognition

No policy endures unless it makes good behaviour sustainable. If we want mentors and mentees to treat guidance as serious work, the profession must reward it in tangible and symbolic ways. Incentives convert values into habits; recognition keeps those habits alive.

1. Linking Mentorship to Continuing Professional Development (CPD)

Every hour spent mentoring should count as an hour of structured learning. The **Nigerian Bar Association** already requires lawyers to accumulate CPD points yearly. The National Mentorship Council can formalise a rule:

- Mentors earn CPD credits for verified sessions and documented feedback.

- Mentees earn CPD credits for completing the mentorship cycle and submitting reflections.

This simple linkage **transforms mentorship from optional philanthropy to part of professional compliance.** Teaching becomes equivalent to study.

2. Linking Recognition to Career Advancement

The **Body of Benchers**, **Judicial Service Commissions**, and **NBA National Secretariat** can integrate mentorship track records into promotion and appointment criteria.

- For **Senior Advocate of Nigeria (SAN)** applications, active mentorship should count toward the "contribution to the legal profession" criterion.

- For judicial appointments, proven mentoring of juniors or clerks should strengthen a candidate's suitability profile.

- For academia, mentorship hours should appear alongside publications during promotion reviews.
  When guidance becomes a currency, its value multiplies.

3. Awards and Public Acknowledgment

People repeat what is celebrated. Annual awards can humanise policy:

- **Mentor of the Year Award** at the NBA Annual General Conference;

- **Judicial Guide Honour** for outstanding bench mentorship;

- **Outstanding Law School Supervisor Recognition** for exemplary externship training;

- **Branch Mentorship Excellence Plaque** for active NBA branches.

The media arm of the NBA can publish short profiles of these honourees. Such visibility dignifies service and encourages others and peers to emulate it.

4. Financial and Institutional Incentives

Mentorship also demands time, and time has economic cost. The system should therefore design light but real incentives that's makes up for this demands on a mentors time:

- Reduced conference fees for accredited mentors;

- Priority access to NBA committees and continuing education grants;

- Tax-deductible recognition for firms that operate structured mentorship programmes (subject to government cooperation).

Even modest gestures such as—reserved seating, certificates, public appreciation—create social prestige that reinforces moral duty.

5. The Value of Symbolic Honour

Not all rewards must be material. A mentor's greatest satisfaction often lies in witnessing the mentee's growth. Institutions can formalise that emotional dividend through symbolic rituals such as: pinning ceremonies for newly certified mentors, letters of appreciation signed by the NMC Chairperson, or digital badges displayed on professional profiles. Visibility is validation.

6. The Reciprocity Principle

A final incentive is moral reciprocity. Every mentee who completes a mentorship cycle should be invited—indeed obliged—to mentor another within three years. The call to pass on knowledge is the profession's own perpetuation design. In time, mentorship will no longer depend on awards; it will become the expected rhythm of belonging.

Principle Five – Monitoring and Evaluation

No system survives on enthusiasm alone. The most elegant framework will erode unless it can see itself—measure its reach, its effect, and its failures for the purpose of adjusting. **Monitoring** and evaluation (M&E) do not exist to punish; they exist to preserve. In mentorship, they ensure that intention turns into impact.

1. The Philosophy of Light Oversight

Lawyers value autonomy, so any monitoring framework must respect dignity while ensuring accountability. The idea is light oversight: gather enough information to detect drift, never so much that it erodes autonomy. We should measure what matters—engagement, diversity, and outcomes—without turning the process into paperwork.

2. Key Performance Indicators (KPIs)

The **National Mentorship Council (NMC)** should publish a short list of measurable indicators each year. Examples include:

- Number of active mentor–mentee pairings per NBA branch.

- Average number of mentorship hours logged.

- Percentage of mentees reporting improved competence and ethics.

- Gender and regional distribution of participation.

- Reduction in disciplinary complaints linked to mentoring interventions.

These metrics will evolve with experience. Whatever is counted will grow.

Technology simplifies integrity: time-stamped entries, auto-generated summaries, and dashboards for analysis reduce subjectivity.

4. Feedback Loops

Evaluation must feed back into learning. The NMC should circulate concise Mentorship Insights Bulletins highlighting best practices and common pitfalls. Institutions can then adapt policies before problems harden. Feedback loops turn monitoring from inspection into mentorship itself..

5. Managing Confidentiality

Monitoring must never expose private conversations. Logs will capture frequency and themes, not content. Ethical oversight committees should ensure that information is used only for improvement, never for sanction without due process. Trust sustains reporting; without it, honesty vanishes.

6. Learning from the Bench

The judiciary already measures performance through case disposal rates (return of cases paradigm) and judgment quality indicators. Similar discipline can be emulated and made to apply in mentorship tracking - revealing how mentorship affects advocacy standards, and courtroom behaviour. The NJI and NMC can jointly publish anonymised records of correlations between mentoring activity and professional outcomes.

7. Continuous Improvement

The M&E framework should remain a living instrument. Every five years the NMC can convene a Mentorship Policy Review Conference—a national dialogue on data, ethics, and evolving needs. Such institutional reflection keeps the framework young.

Principle Six – Inclusivity and Equity

A mentorship system that excludes is not merely incomplete; it is unjust. The law exists to equalise opportunity, yet our profession sometimes mirrors the very inequalities it is meant to correct. Institutionalising mentorship gives us a rare chance to redress those imbalances—not through rhetoric, but through deliberate design.

1. Why Inclusivity Matters

Mentorship is more than skill transfer; it is affirmation. To be chosen, listened to, and guided tells a young lawyer, "You belong here." For women, persons with disabilities, and lawyers from underrepresented regions, that affirmation can determine whether they stay in the profession or quietly exit it. Equity in mentorship is therefore both moral duty and strategic necessity. A diverse Bar strengthens public confidence in justice.

2. Gender Representation

The gender gap in senior legal positions remains pronounced. Few women reach partnership in large firms or appointment to the higher Bench, not for lack of talent, but often for lack of sponsorship. The mentorship framework must therefore include:

- **Dedicated Women's Mentorship Network** under the NBA Women Forum, pairing senior female practitioners with upcoming female lawyers.

- **Monitoring Gender Ratios** in mentorship participation, with branches encouraged to maintain a minimum of 40% female mentee representation.
  When the pipeline is widened, diversity flows naturally.

3. Regional and Socio-Economic Equity

Not all branches of the NBA have equal access to mentors. Urban centres overflow with seniors; rural branches starve of them. The National Mentorship Council (NMC) should balance this disparity through **Cluster Mentorships(see previous chapters on this)**—digital or rotational programmes linking mentors from metropolitan branches to mentees in underserved regions. Virtual platforms can bridge geography. Equity begins with access.

4. Inclusion of Persons with Disabilities

Lawyers living with disabilities often face both architectural and attitudinal barriers. The mentorship policy must ensure:

- accessible digital platforms;

- priority pairing with mentors who understand adaptive practice;

- inclusion of disability-awareness modules in mentor training.

A profession that excludes voices of resilience deprives itself of wisdom.

5. Generational Inclusion

Inclusivity also means welcoming new energy. Younger mentors—lawyers with five to nine years post-call experience—should not be excluded. They can guide peers through immediate practical challenges while learning from seniors as well: in a - mentor, mentee, mentor again - construct. This tiered approach multiplies capacity and ensures continuity.

6. Institutional Partnerships for Inclusion

The NMC can collaborate with:

- **National Human Rights Commission, Federal Ministry of Women Affairs**, and **Joint National Association of Persons with Disabilities (JONAPWD)** to integrate inclusion standards.

- **Corporate donors and NGOs may be approached** to sponsor scholarships and travel support for mentees with disabilities or from disadvantaged backgrounds.

Equity thrives when partnerships share its cost.

7. The Culture Shift

True inclusion requires more than policies. It demands daily acts of consideration and respect: seniors consciously inviting younger voices to speak; juniors acknowledging that equality is sustained by participation, not entitlement. The inclusive mentorship culture is not a project; it is a habit of respect.

Principle Seven – Sustainability and Funding

Every good reform is tested not by its birth but by its endurance. Mentorship initiatives have risen and fallen with each Bar administration because their lifeblood—resources and continuity—was never secured. Sustainability is not merely about money; it is about structure, system, ownership, and foresight.

1. Shared Ownership, Shared Funding

Mentorship belongs to the whole profession; therefore, its costs should be distributed. The **National Mentorship Council (NMC)** should draw funding from multiple streams:

- **Core Contributions** from institutional partners

- **Partnership Grants** from development agencies and corporate sponsors interested in justice reform.

- **Modest Participation Fees** for elective programmes (not for basic mentorship, which remains free).

- **Government Support** through the Federal Ministry of Justice and state ministries under their access-to-justice budgets.

The goal is not dependency but resilience: when no single donor controls the purse, the mission survives.

2. Administrative Efficiency

The NMC secretariat must operate leanly: a small professional team using technology to reduce cost. Automation—digital forms, dashboards, and virtual meetings—cuts expenses. Transparency in accounting ensures credibility; all reports should be publicly accessible on the Council's website.

3. Building Institutional Memory

Funding continuity requires institutional memory. The NMC should maintain a Mentorship Legacy Archive—a digital repository of frameworks, reports, and best practices. Each new leadership begins where the last stopped, not from scratch. Knowledge is the cheapest form of sustainability.

4. Integration into Existing Budgets

Mentorship does not need an entirely new financial ecosystem; it needs presence and visibility within existing ones. The NBA's Annual General Conference budget can set aside 5% for mentorship sessions and awards. The NJI can dedicate a fixed slot in its training calendar for mentorship modules. The Law School can integrate supervision training into its faculty development plan. Embedding these will prevent their omission.

5. Incentivising Private-Sector Support

Corporate law firms and institutions benefit directly from well-mentored lawyers. The NBA can create a **Mentorship - Sponsorship Scheme** that allows firms to contribute to mentorship programmes in exchange for public recognition and CPD privileges. Sponsorship with transparency transforms philanthropy into partnership.

6. Legal Backing for Financial Predictability

Eventually, mentorship funding would have to be secured through a brief statutory provision—perhaps inserted into the Legal Practitioners Act or an NBA by-law—authorising the Council to collect and manage funds independently, subject to annual audit. **Law gives permanence where policy alone cannot.**

7. Succession Planning

Sustainability also concerns people. Each mentorship body—branch committees, law faculties, judicial divisions—should have vice-chairs or deputies groomed to succeed. Training-the-trainers programmes ensure that expertise regenerates. **Innovations die not from lack of money, but from lack of stewards.**

Designing for Endurance

Institutionalising mentorship is not a one-time reform; it is the quiet work of generations. What I have outlined is a framework capable of surviving political cycles and evolving with the profession's needs. Its durability rests on governance, standards, integration, incentives, measurement, equity, and sustainability—the seven pillars of a living system.

The architecture is ready; what remains is will. If the Nigerian legal profession adopts this blueprint in earnest, mentorship will cease to be a lament and become our legacy. The next chapter will turn from design to practice—how to implement this framework step by step across institutions, beginning with the pilot phase.

CHAPTER SIX

Implementation and Pilot Programmes — From Blueprint to Action

Introduction – From Design to Doing

Blueprints inspire; implementation transforms. The test of any reform is not applause at its launch but the quiet efficiency of its execution. After years of speeches and policy papers, what the legal profession now needs is a road map—one that specifies who does what, when, and with what resources. This chapter provides that path.

I write not as an architect of theory nor as a custodian of process but he following framework is deliberately practical and It assumes the limited budgets, overlapping mandates, and political transitions that often derail reforms in Nigeria. Its aim is simple: to create a mentorship system that begins modestly, proves value, then scales sustainably.

The Pilot Programme (Year One)

The pilot stage is where aspiration meets reality. Its goal is to test structure, tools, and incentives in a controlled environment before national rollout.

1. Duration and Scope

- **Timeline:** 12 months

- **Pilot Regions:** Lagos, Abuja (FCT), Kano, Enugu, Port Harcourt, and one northern and one middle-belt state for diversity.

- **Institutions Involved:** NBA branches, Law School campuses, NJI, and two law faculties per region.

- **Participants:** 500 mentors and 1,500 mentees across all zones.

2. Administrative Setup

- The **National Mentorship Council (NMC)** appoints a Pilot Implementation Committee (PIC) chaired by a Court of Appeal Justice.

- Each pilot zone establishes a Zonal Mentorship Desk within its NBA branch office.

- The PIC coordinates training of mentors, monitors activities, and compiles data.

3. Key Activities

1. **Mentor Accreditation Workshops** – three-day sessions on ethics, communication, and feedback.

2. **Pairing and Orientation** – digital matching through the National Mentorship Registry; induction webinars for mentees.

3. **Monthly Engagements** – structured one-hour meetings or joint case reviews.

4. **Quarterly Reports** – brief electronic submissions summarising progress.

5. **Mid-Year Review Conference** – cross-regional meeting to share lessons and adjust templates.

6. **Final Evaluation** – independent report detailing participation rates, satisfaction, and early outcomes.

4. Outputs

- Tested mentorship software.

- Refined reporting templates.

- Baseline data for national rollout.

- Early success stories for communication and encouragement.

5. Budget Estimate (Pilot Year)

Item	Estimated Cost (₦ million)	Funding Source
Mentor Workshops (7 regions)	--	NBA/NJI
Registry Platform & Hosting	--	NMC Secretariat
Stipends for Pilot Coordination	--	CLE/NBA
Monitoring & Evaluation	--	Donor grants
Communication & Awards	--	Private sponsorship
Total	**-- million**	

Even modest funding can launch a credible pilot scheme when partnerships share the cost.

National Rollout (Years Two–Three)

Once the pilot scheme validates tools and methods, expansion can begin.

1. Scale-Up Plan

- Extend mentorship to all **NBA branches** and **Law School campuses**.

- Integrate mentorship into **judicial induction** at NJI and **law faculty externships** nationwide.

- Establish the **National Mentorship Registry** as a permanent platform.

2. Implementation Steps

1. **Training of Trainers (TOT):** each pilot mentor trains five new mentors.

2. **Branch Integration:** mentorship committees embedded in every NBA branch.

3. **Institutional Memoranda:** formal MoU's among NBA, CLE, NJI, and Body of Benchers.

4. **Public Launch:** national inauguration event to announce full rollout.

5. **Ongoing Evaluation:** annual State of Mentorship Report published by the NMC.

3. Expected Outputs

- At least 10,000 mentor–mentee pairings nationwide.

- Mentorship counted for CPD credits in all branches.

- Integration into legal education accreditation standards.

Phase Three: Consolidation and Continuous Improvement (Years Four–Five)

By this stage, mentorship becomes a professional norm rather than a project.

Institutionalize Measures

- Embed mentorship metrics in **NBA elections** and **Judicial promotions**.

- Include mentorship compliance in **firm accreditation** and **law faculty reviews**.

- NMC evolves from programme oversight to quality assurance and innovation.

Operational Instruments and Templates

1. **Mentorship Agreement Form** – captures names, objectives, confidentiality, and duration.

2. **Monthly Log Template** – date, topic, key lessons, next steps.

3. **Evaluation Form** – 10-question survey for both mentor and mentee.

4. **Branch Summary Sheet** – one-page quarterly data submission.

5. **Annual Audit Checklist** – participation rates, gender ratio, and satisfaction scores.
   Digital forms will be hosted on the NMC portal, printable for branches even without reliable internet.

Budget Framework and Resource Planning

Cost Centre	Annual Estimate (₦ million)	Responsible Institution
NMC Secretariat & Staff	--	NMC Core Budget
Registry Platform Maintenance	--	NBA/NMC
Training & CPD Integration	--	CLE/NJI
Regional Coordination	--	NBA Branches
Evaluation & Research	--	Donor Grants/Partners
Communication & Recognition	--	Private Sponsors
Total Estimated Annual Cost	-- million	

These is merely illustrative; what matters is proportional contribution and transparency.

Implementation Risks and Mitigation

Risk	Likely Impact	Mitigation
High Leadership turnover	Loss of continuity	Embed mentorship in constitutions and by-laws
Funding shortfall	Interrupted programmes	Multi-source funding and reserve fund
Data fatigue	Inaccurate reporting	Simplified digital tools and incentives
Cultural resistance	Low participation	Early success stories, recognition, and CPD credits
Abuse of mentorship	Ethical breaches	Clear and defined Charter and ethics committees

Measuring Success by Continuity

When the pilot matures into habit, mentorship will cease to be rhetorics; it will become the normal rhythm of the Bar. True success will not be in numbers but in the change of narrative— junior lawyers speaking of seniors who shaped their minds, judges tracing their discipline to mentors, and citizens sensing a humane, balanced, and steadier justice system.

Institutionalisation is not a single act or effort of reform; it is the creation of a living system that keeps correcting and adjusting itself. Once that culture is in motion, it will need little defence. Mentorship will have found its home.

CHAPTER SEVEN

The Future of Mentorship — Sustaining Professional Excellence

Introduction — The Road Beyond Reform

The purpose of policy is not perfection but progress. Institutionalising mentorship, as mapped in this book, will not cure every ailment of our profession, but it will strengthen the sinews that hold the body together. Implementation is the first half of success; endurance is the other. This chapter sets out how we, as a profession, can protect the reforms once they begin—by embedding mentorship in law, culture, and leadership succession.

Legislative and Regulatory Consolidation

1. Legal Codification

A reform that depends only on goodwill dies when goodwill wanes. The next legislative milestone should be the **Legal Practitioners (Amendment) Bill on Mentorship and Professional Development**, proposed jointly by the Nigerian Bar Association (NBA) and the Body of Benchers. The Bill would:

- Recognise mentorship as a statutory duty of every legal practitioner.

- Establish the **National Mentorship Council (NMC)** as a body corporate with perpetual succession.

- Authorise the NMC to issue mentorship guidelines, maintain a registry, and levy modest fees for sustainability.

- Require periodic reports to the Attorney-General of the Federation and National Assembly.

Until such legislation is passed, interim authority may derive from amendments to the Rules of Professional Conduct (2023) and formal MoUs among the NBA, NJI, and CLE.

2. Harmonisation of Regulations

Each institution must revise its own internal regulations to align with the national framework:

- The **Council of Legal Education** updates the Law School Manual to include mentorship assessment.

- The **NBA Constitution** creates a permanent Mentorship Directorate.

- The **National Judicial Institute Act** incorporates mentorship as a statutory function under continuing judicial education.

- Law faculties integrate mentorship evaluation into their accreditation reviews by the National Universities

Commission (NUC).

Legislative alignment converts parallel streams into a single river.

Strategic Leadership and Institutional Continuity

1. The Role of the Chief Justice of Nigeria

As head of the legal profession, the Chief Justice can anchor mentorship in national consciousness by issuing an annual Mentorship Policy Directive, echoing what the Chief Justice's Policy Directions achieved for case management. Each new directive would reaffirm standards, review progress, and set targets for the year.

2. The Role of the Nigerian Bar Association

The NBA should institutionalise a **Mentorship Transition Protocol**: when one administration ends, the incoming leadership must receive a handover report and pledge to maintain existing programmes for at least one year before review. This single clause can end the cycle of constant reinvention.

3. The Role of Law Faculties and the Council of Legal Education

Universities must view mentorship as a component of accreditation. The CLE can require evidence of faculty-led mentorship structures when renewing law faculty approvals. Faculties that demonstrate excellence may be recognised as

Mentorship Centers of Excellence—bridging the academy and the Bar.

4. The Role of the National Judicial Institute

The NJI should host an annual Judicial Mentorship Symposium bringing together judges, academics, and practitioners to share lessons across generations. Such forums refresh both content and commitment.

Public–Private Partnerships and International Cooperation

Mentorship strengthens rule of law, and rule of law attracts development. The **NMC** should cultivate partnerships with:

- **Development partners** (UNDP, British Council, GIZ) for technical assistance and digital infrastructure.

- **Corporate organisations** for sponsorship of scholarships and awards.

- **Foreign Bars** (UK, Canada, South Africa, Kenya) for exchange programs and setting benchmarks.

International collaboration broadens perspective and enhances credibility in global legal rankings.

Data, Research, and Innovation

Mentorship must evolve with technology and society. The National Mentorship Council should establish a **Mentorship Research Unit** to:

- Analyze data from the National Registry and produce annual analytical reports.

- Partner with law faculties for empirical research on mentorship's impact on professional ethics and client satisfaction.

- Innovate to produce digital tools—AI-assisted feedback systems, mentorship analytics dashboards, and e-learning modules etc.

Evidence-based policy will keep the framework responsive and prevent stagnation.

Ethics, Accountability, and Disciplinary Integration

Reform without integrity is performance. To protect mentorship from abuse:

- The **NMC Ethics Code** must prohibit exploitation, harassment, or discrimination within mentoring relationships.

- Breaches will be reported to the NBA Disciplinary Committee or Judicial Service Commission, depending on status.

- Every mentee will have access to confidential grievance channels.

The profession's moral authority rests on the trust that mentorship relationships are safe and honourable.

Financing the Future

Sustainability requires predictable funding streams. Over the next decade, the NMC should:

- Establish a **Mentorship Endowment Fund**, managed transparently and audited annually.

- Secure line items within the budgets of the NBA, NJI, and CLE.

- Continue engaging corporate sponsors under clear ethical guidelines.

- Introduce a small levy—no more than ₦1,000 per practising lawyer annually—earmarked solely for mentorship development.

A transparent, independently audited system will preserve credibility and protect the programme from political volatility.

Evaluation and Global Benchmarking

Every five years, Nigeria's mentorship system should undergo an external audit by a Commonwealth peer institution—perhaps the Law Society of Kenya or the Bar Standards Board of England and Wales. International peer review will identify gaps, strengthen legitimacy, and sustain excellence. The report's summary should be published publicly; transparency is the mother of accountability.

The Duty of Continuity

The legal profession endures because it regenerates itself. If this mentorship framework is implemented with discipline, Nigeria will, within a decade, possess not only more competent lawyers but a more civil justice system—one where learning is shared, not hoarded. The architecture we have designed is not ornamental; it is functional. It belongs to every chamber, every courtroom, every classroom.

I close this work with a simple conviction: law is a living trust. We inherit it from those before us, and we are obliged to improve it for those who follow. Institutionalising mentorship is how we keep that trust. If we do it well, posterity will not remember us for what we built, but for whom we prepared.

Institutionalising Mentorship in the Legal Profession: A Strategic Blueprint for Professional Development by Hon. Justice Mabel Segun Bello

Author's Final Note and Acknowledgment of Partners

I have walked long enough within the corridors of justice to know that no single mind builds a system. This work was born not of solitude but of fellowship—of conversations with colleagues, friends, clerks, academics, and students who still believe that excellence can be taught as well as required.

I am greatly indebted to the immense contributions of Amb. Samson Tobi Bolarin whose research tenacity and extensive encouragement propelled me greatly to the finishing line of this book.

I am grateful to the **Nigerian Bar Association**, whose continuing dialogue on professional renewal inspired many of these proposals; to the **Council of Legal Education** and the **Nigerian Law School**, for opening their classrooms to reform; and to the **National Judicial Institute**, for reminding us that mentorship on the Bench is the surest defense of public confidence. My thanks also go to the countless young lawyers I have encountered, whose questions sharpened my answer and partly inspired this book.

Special thanks and appreciation to the **JOHNNY AGIM, SAN FOUNDATION** – (The JASAN Foundation), whose patriotic zeal on matters of structured mentorship in the legal profession, serve as a great motivation and inspiration for the title, structure and content of this book.

To every mentor who still takes the time to guide another, I offer respect. To every mentee who listens, reflects, and then teaches in turn, I offer hope. You are the living proof that tradition can modernise without losing its soul.

May this book serve as both blueprint and bridge—linking what we were to what we must become. The future of our profession will not be written in decrees, but in the daily patience of those who choose to teach. If we each take one hand and lift it, mentorship will cease to be rhetorics; it will become our culture.

— **Hon. Justice Mabel T. Segun-Bello**
Federal High Court of Nigeria
October 2025

Table of References

A. Statutes and Rules

1. Legal Practitioners Act, Cap L11, Laws of the Federation of Nigeria (2004).

2. Legal Education (Consolidation, etc.) Act, Cap L10, Laws of the Federation of Nigeria (2004).

3. Rules of Professional Conduct for Legal Practitioners (2023).

4. Constitution of the Federal Republic of Nigeria (1999, as amended).

5. Legal Practice Act No. 28 of 2014 (Republic of South Africa).

6. Bar Standards Board Handbook (United Kingdom, 2023).

7. Law Society of Ontario Rules of Professional Conduct (Canada, 2022).

8. Law Society of Kenya (Training and Pupillage) Regulations (2019).

9. Legal Profession Uniform Admission Rules (Australia, 2015).

B. Institutional and Policy Documents

1. National Judicial Institute Act (Cap N55, LFN 2004) and NJI Annual Reports (2020–2024).

2. Nigerian Bar Association Constitution (as amended, 2022).

3. Nigerian Law School Students' Handbook (Council of Legal Education, 2023).

4. Young Lawyers' Forum Mentorship Framework (Nigerian Bar Association, 2021).

5. National Universities Commission Benchmark Minimum Academic Standards for Law (BMAS, 2022 Edition).

6. Body of Benchers Guidelines on Call to the Bar and Ethics (Revised 2023).

7. NULAI Nigeria Clinical Legal Education Standards (2018).

8. Mentorship and Continuing Professional Development Guidelines (Law Society of Ontario, 2021).

9. Bar Council Mentoring Scheme Handbook (England and Wales, 2020).

10. Legal Practice Council Strategic Plan (South Africa, 2021–2025).

C. Books and Scholarly Works

1. Adekunle, T. (2020). Professional Ethics and the Nigerian Bar: A Historical Analysis. Lagos: Malthouse Press.

2. Ajayi, F. (2019). Law in Practice: Ethics, Advocacy and Mentorship in Nigeria. Ibadan: Spectrum Books.

3. Elias, T.O. (1972). The Nigerian Legal System. London: Routledge.

4. Cownie, F. (2017). Legal Academics: Culture and Identities. Oxford: Hart Publishing.

5. Twining, W. (1994). Blackstone's Tower: The English Law School. London: Stevens.

6. Nzelibe, C. (2021). "Professional Socialisation and Legal Ethics in Africa," African Journal of Legal Studies, Vol. 14(2).

7. Latham, J. (2020). Mentorship in the Legal Profession: Building Capacity and Culture. Cambridge University

Press.

8. Mutunga, W. (2015). Transformative Constitutionalism in Kenya: The Theory and the Practice. Nairobi: Strathmore University Press.

9. Thornton, M. (2016). Privatising the Public University: The Case of Law. New York: Routledge.

10. Bello, M.S. (2025). Institutionalising Mentorship in the Legal Profession: A Strategic Blueprint for Professional Development. Abuja: [Publisher].

D. Reports, Articles, and Online Publications

1. Nigerian Bar Association (NBA). Mentorship: A Tool for Professional Development. Report of the 2022 Annual General Conference.

2. Premium Times (2023). "Mentorship Gaps and the Future of Legal Practice in Nigeria."

3. ThisDay Law (2024). "Bridging the Generational Divide at the Bar."

4. The Guardian Nigeria (2022). "Young Lawyers and the Challenge of Professional Guidance."

5. The Punch Editorial (2023). "Mentorship and Ethics in Nigeria's Legal System."

6. LawCare UK (2021). "The Wellbeing Case for Mentoring in Law."

7. Canadian Bar Association (2020). "Mentoring Across Generations: Building Resilient Lawyers."

8. Legal Resources Foundation (Kenya, 2019). Report on Structured Pupillage Implementation.

9. World Bank Group (2020). Strengthening Judicial Education and Legal Professional Development in Africa.

10. United Nations Development Programme (UNDP). Rule of Law and Access to Justice in Nigeria: Policy Brief 2022.

E. Comparative International References

1. Bar Standards Board (UK) — Pupillage Supervision Handbook (2021).

2. Law Society of Ontario — Mentorship and Articling Resources (2023).

3. Legal Practice Council (South Africa) — Code of Conduct and Supervision Framework (2020).

4. Law Society of Kenya — Annual Report on Professional Standards (2022).

5. Victorian Bar (Australia) — New Barristers' Mentoring Programme Manual (2019).

6. Commonwealth Lawyers Association — Mentoring for the Next Generation: Regional Policy Paper (2021).

7. International Bar Association (IBA) — Global Report on Mentorship and Wellbeing in the Legal Profession (2022).

8. UN Office on Drugs and Crime (UNODC) — Global Judicial Integrity Network: Mentorship Toolkit (2023).

F. Digital and Online Legal Resources

1. https://www.nigerianbar.org.ng — Nigerian Bar Association official portal.

2. https://nji.gov.ng — National Judicial Institute.

3. https://www.lawschool.gov.ng — Council of Legal Education / Nigerian Law School.

4. https://www.barcouncil.org.uk — Bar Council of England and Wales.

5. https://www.lawsociety.ca — Law Society of Ontario.

6. https://www.lsk.or.ke — Law Society of Kenya.

7. https://www.lpc.org.za — Legal Practice Council, South Africa.

8. https://www.commonwealthlawyers.com — Commonwealth Lawyers Association.

www.ingramcontent.com/pod-product-compliance
Lightning Source LLC
Chambersburg PA
CBHW080134270326
41926CB00021B/4485